Vivienne Westwood

First published in Great Britain in 1997
by Thames and Hudson Ltd, London

Copyright © 1997 Éditions Assouline, Paris

British Library Cataloguing-in-Publication Data
A catalogue record for this book is available from
the British Library

ISBN 0-500-01786-7

Printed and bound in Italy

Vivienne Westwood

Text by Gene Krell

Thames and Hudson

I have a world of images of women in Westwood: smiles, glances, moving images – 'Poetry in Motion'. In the early Eighties I was managing Vivienne's World's End shop. It was the time of the magnificent 'Nostalgia of Mud' collection, with its huge wool skirts, mini sheepskin jackets, ten-gallon hats and bag shoes. We had all types of people coming in, some out of sheer curiosity. One busy Saturday morning this Italian-American woman came by. Recently widowed, she had been left a great deal of money and had decided to travel to ease her loss.

Although she was familiar with Vivienne's name and work through the Press, she had never actually seen the clothes. She was beautifully dressed in beige cashmere and her initial reaction was shock. But we began to talk and I encouraged her to try some things on. She was immediately transfixed and engaged and went on to buy from the collection.

Later that afternoon, I went off to Smile, a popular hairdresser in the posh Knightsbridge section of London, to get my hair cut. As I entered the salon, one of the assistants beckoned: 'Come to the window!', and there she was in the street. The same woman, completely transformed: proud, noble, beautiful and confident in all these Buffalo clothes. I was pleased and reassured to see her believing in her own power. Westwood's ideas have the ability to move people, to rouse and stir them. The sheer glamour of the clothes can hold one hostage.

Then there was a Japanese girl who telephoned before she came to England to order a Harris tweed suit with mini crini and all accessories and arranged for a photographer to take her picture clad in her new toilette outside the shop.

Recently I saw an older woman, understated in style, with flat shoes and a good classic skirt. She too is radiant, for it is the detail on the collar, the buttons, the turn of a cuff that make her blouse so special, so Westwood. The signature is there, unmistakable. This is the mark of genius few designers possess.

•

I first set eyes on Vivienne Westwood in 1969 – an unforgettable moment. She had blond spikey hair and was dressed in tight leopard-print velvet trousers and black patent stiletto boots with pointed toes. Her style dazzled me and when you are dazzled you investigate.

Our first conversation was about Rock 'n' Roll music and its roots in America.

Interest in the Fifties was just beginning to emerge. William Klein's 1969 film *Mr Freedom* had parodied the American myth of Superman. Tommy Roberts took the name 'Mr Freedom' for his shop at 430, King's Road and began selling American pop culture of the Forties and Fifties as fashion; Mickey Mouse was chic. Vivienne tells me this is where she bought her leopard trousers.

When 'Mr Freedom' moved to a bigger shop in Kensington, he had a shop assistant called Harold, a working-class kid dressed straight out of the Fifties in teddy-boy suit and crepe-sole shoes. Malcolm McLaren, Vivienne's boyfriend, also wore these shoes, along with satin cowboy shirts and lurex drainpipe trousers made by Vivienne.

tommy Roberts's partner, Trevor Myles, kept the shop at 430, King's Road and turned it into Paradise Garage, the first shop in England to sell used denim. But it was not long before Myles's interest waned – he became preoccupied with the high life and showcasing his new Swedish bombshell wife – and in 1970 he invited Malcolm and Vivienne to use the back area of the shop. There they sold second-hand Fifties records and memorabilia and old radios collected from flea markets. Then Myles turned over the entire shop to them and they added some unused stocks of Fifties clothes and four newly made teddy-boy suits. Vivienne started to take clothes apart in order to copy them. They called the shop Let It Rock.

this return to the Fifties at a time when everyone seemed to have settled for flared trousers and platform shoes marked the beginning of the age of nostalgia for our generation. Malcolm, who had just finished art school, hoped to attract trendy kids – one of the first customers was Charlie Saatchi (of the famous PR company), then avid for old records. Strange as it may now seem, Fifties music was never played on the radio in those days but there was a growing interest in the period and Elvis was already making his comeback. What Malcolm hadn't foreseen was that there was a whole wave of second-time-around teddy boys, like Harold, frequenting the pubs in the East End of London and around the country. These came to Let It Rock in droves; the ones from up north hired coaches.

it was at this time that our friendship began to flourish. Initially, it was not terribly easy, and I understood their suspicion of not only me, but my business. I had a shop, further down the road, called Granny Takes A Trip, which sold slim-cut velvet rhinestone suits with flared trousers, and androgynous fashion, to pop icons like David Bowie and Mick Jagger, exponents of what history would come to view as Glam Rock.

In a sense, I was in the enemy camp. In velvet suits, high-heeled patchwork boots, and with long dyed black hair, I seemed to have little to do with their reality. Malcolm was such a character, portraying himself as this street-smart Ted, while discussing Dadaist art. I have never encountered a more diverse mentality, or such a Walter Mittyish existence.

Vivienne was another matter: so stunning, so incredibly stunning, with a lovely curvaceous body, beautifully shaped athletic legs, and an intense manner of speaking. I was so taken with her that I no longer considered what they thought of me. Knowing that they loved the Fifties, I invited them over to my house to watch the classic film *The Blackboard Jungle*.

●

I knew this was a strange getting together since they detested everything they felt I stood for. The hippy movement, which had arisen out of protest against the corruption of the power elite, had started to make us question what we were told but these two saw Flower Power as a cop-out to the older generation whose marketeers were already mass-manufacturing it as a lifestyle: the world of

Peace and Love seemed determined by a boring round of free music festivals and drug taking.

They hated the older generation and related more to a James Dean image. Yet what happened to hippy fashion eventually happened to Malcolm and Vivienne – their ideas right up to and including punk and post-punk became sucked into the establishment. Even attitude gets marketed – look what has happened to James Dean.

Paradoxically enough, they functioned as a family unit; Vivienne had a son by her marriage to Derek Westwood (she kept the name), and a son with Malcolm. Vivienne and Malcolm had met while she was teaching school and he was a university student. She is five years his senior. What bound them together was that they were rebels. They saw their rebellion as one of youth against age and they invaded fashion with a new and envenomed form of this credo. It reconstituted every notion we had about ourselves and the way we looked so that I started to shift my own belief system and eventually grew close to the two of them.

The fact that Vivienne no longer believes that youthful disgust will automatically produce change and that without real ideas – that is, ideas formed from a perspective of knowledge and experience – no beneficial change can occur, suggests that even at this stage this credo had its weak points.

Seeing the limitations of teddy boys, the two moved towards rockers and black urban culture. In 1972 they redecorated the shop and changed its name to Too Fast To Live, Too Young To Die; it now sold lots of leather with chains and zips, as well as zoot suits – a popular style among Black Americans in the Fifties. They had already started to sell T-shirts printed with pornographic images and when in 1974 they were prosecuted for this under the obscenity laws their reaction was to change the name of the shop again, this time to Sex, and produce images that were even more hard-core. (This is one idea that has not yet been sucked into the establishment mainstream.) Now they added S&M clothing – 'rubberwear for the office', Malcolm called it – and torn clothes. Vivienne was walking down the street in leather mini skirts wound round with chains and padlocks, T-shirts with holes, ripped fishnets and stilettos, or rubber negligees and rubber stockings: nobody had seen anything like it – she stopped the traffic.

meanwhile Malcolm was in America managing the New York Dolls, whom he'd met as customers when they came to the shop. He liaised by telephone with Vivienne and she made their stage clothes. Malcolm had encouraged the 'Dolls' to spout Maoist rhetoric in the hope of annoying the Americans, so the clothes were all made in red materials, including red rubber and vinyl.

When the 'Dolls' folded Malcolm returned to Vivienne. Her latest design was an anarchy shirt – distressed to look old, with bleached-out stripes, and appliquéd with badges, flags and slogans: 'Only Anarchists are Pretty!', 'Dangerously close to Love', 'We are not afraid of Ruins', 'Chaos', and a woven label from Chinatown of the portrait of Karl Marx, to which Malcolm added a swastika. This shirt looked as if it belonged to an urban guerrilla and Malcolm saw in it the key to a new collection of clothes. All the current themes – rips, zips, porn, slogans, bondage and chains – were pressed into service and punk style was born. But not yet launched. The shop had to be given a new decor and a new name. While Vivienne continued to work on the clothes, Malcolm succumbed to the pestering of his young mate and most stylish customer, Steve Jones, who wanted him to manage his pop group. They asked a young kid with green hair called John Lydon to audition to the shop's juke box. As lead singer he became Johnny Rotten. Malcolm called the group Sex Pistols.

rotten put a safety pin through his ear and, wearing the new punk clothes, the Sex Pistols played their first gig in 1976. Then the shop, Seditionaries, opened, to immediate cult status.

The Sex Pistols seemed to represent the culmination of all that Malcolm and Vivienne had come to signify. They were every mother's nightmare and the voice of a generation. In an effort to repress them, the BBC refused to play their number one song, 'God Save the Queen'. Vivienne has never had a better vehicle for her designs and ideas on style.

Vivienne was punk's prototype and greatest showpiece. Her style at this point was extraordinary – platinum blonde spiked hair, pale skin with dark lipstick, and wonderful little mini kilts with outsized bondage boots. All you could do was stop and reassess what you found aesthetically pleasing. She completely possessed you.

Punk was such a powerful statement. Kids were dyeing their hair pink, green, purple, putting safety pins through their cheeks, wearing chains and spikes. 'Punk' and 'Anarchy' read the graffiti on the walls.

All of this had a commercial viability, and punk soon hit the department stores, sold to mothers who made sure their children were in the house by 9 p.m. Its impact on high fashion was revolutionary. It revealed that McLaren and Westwood had an enormous capacity to understand the culture of their time.

The collapse of the Sex Pistols and its aftermath left Vivienne with no nostalgia for punk. She began technical research into historical dress and with Malcolm she referred to the past for ideas: everything from Native Americans to social outcasts and rebels. They came up with the idea of pirates, 'Romantics of the High Seas'. This marked a radical departure in approach. The collection was filled with wonderful colour and fabric. It was light and textured. It was about gold and treasure, about adventure and exploration. Vivienne had styled her hair in henna ringlets and wrapped her teeth in gold cigarette paper. She was bound now not in chains, but by yards of lovely ikat fabric.

I n 1981, the two presented their first runway show. It seemed as if everything had come full circle. It was just so imaginative, and as dramatic as anything they had done in the past. The styling was exquisite in its detail and the models carried Walkmans and danced to Malcolm's mix of ethnic and rap music. Princess Diana had just become engaged to Charles, and Bernadine Morris of the *New York Times* hailed the London season as 'The Princess and the Pirates'.

This is when Vivienne began to do something unique in fashion. It is usual to suggest the romance of a previous age by superimposing details from past fashions onto the standard system of cutting now in use. Vivienne went to the dynamic source of old garments and copied their cuts in toile (cheap calico); she adopted and reinterpreted these original principles into her patterns and made them modern. This is the foundation of her distinctive technique in the manipulation of materials, not only in the elegant but in the sexual rapport that her clothes have with the body. She feels that as long as there is the past to explore, she can never run out of ideas.

At this time, Vivienne's life and career had reached a turning point. Though her working relationship with Malcolm would last another two years, the two grew further apart, Malcolm involving himself with Adam Ant, managing Bow Wow Wow and going on to launch his solo career.

each of Vivienne's collections has had a title and concept; all have introduced new ideas. Some in particular have redefined her vision as a designer. In 1984, at the height of power dressing, Vivienne's inclination was towards a more feminine power. For her 'Mini Crini' collection of 1984 she chose models with big busts and emphasized the small waist by drawing attention to the hips with a short swinging crinoline or puffball skirt. She reduced the shoulder to its natural size; for this she focused on the classic proportions of English tailoring, using princess lines which could be worn over the crini. It was with this collection that English tailoring became the base of her work. Pornographic innuendo – Page-3-type women dressed as children – was underscored by childish platform clogs.

Vivienne was no longer interested exclusively in the young. As far as the young girl is concerned, the Westwood style now is that she should dress older than her years. I agree with her that there is nothing more sexy than a young girl dressed as a young lady.

The 'Portrait' collection of 1990 has a particular resonance for Vivienne. The models in their platform shoes with 10-inch heels could have stepped out of a painting. There was a logic to the qualities of the fabrics whereby each seemed the epitome of its type, replicating the way a painter selects elements of dress for his portraits. She took the environment within the framed space of a portrait and added the clothes to it: in London's Wallace Collection she discovered a brass inlay design on the back of an eighteenth-century mirror by the furniture designer André-Charles Boulle which she translated into a gold foil print for black velvet dresses; to represent landscape background she used a special tweed of subtle patchwork design in which every square was of a different weave and colour harmony. The final triumph was a photographic print of a Boucher painting from the Wallace Collection: *A Shepherd Watching a Sleeping Shepherdess* ('I just love the pink bow round the sheep's neck,' she said.) This she used both as a shawl and on the front panel of her famous corsets.

Vivienne looks back with love to this collection because it demonstrates so clearly the effect on her work of her great friendship with Gary Bayle.

Gary designed sets for a theatre company in Canada. Then, in the Fifties, he won a scholarship to the Beaux-Arts and became a portrait painter. Vivienne met him in 1977 when he was working with Sir Roland Penrose, re-editing his books, in particular Penrose's book on Picasso. He has spent most of his life reading and is a scholar of cultural criticism.

It was Gary who introduced Vivienne to the Wallace Collection twenty years ago and since then they have met each week for conversations that have fertilized her imagination and intellect.

It is the intellectual quality that she brings to her work which sets her apart from other designers. She *is* unorthodox – she must have been born that way – but it is her self-discipline that makes her original. Her attitude is pagan: anything worth doing is worth doing well; when there is substance, then life can be a pleasure.

All this is very French. Look at the titles of some of her most recent collections: 'On Liberty' (subtitle: 'Le mieux est l'ennemie du bien'), 'Erotic Zones', 'Vive la Cocotte', 'Vive la Bagatelle' – she adores the flirtation of the French eighteenth and nineteenth centuries.

Vivienne is convinced that fashion is the result of the exchange of ideas between France and England (since the seventeenth century the French have been mad about English fashion – she called one collection 'Anglomania'). She explains, 'On the English side we have tailoring and an easy charm, on the French side that solidity of design and proportion that comes from never being satisfied because something can always be done to make it better, more refined – hence an elaboration that always stops short of vulgarity – and then that "je ne sais quoi", the touch that pulls it all together.'

Backstage, helping to dress for the 'Portrait' collection, was a young man, Andreas Kronthaler. He is now Vivienne's husband and shares her work. Together, in the collections 'Erotic Zones' and 'Vive la Cocotte' (1995), they achieved a new silhouette, extreme and incredible in this age of dressing down. I remember Naomi, Tatiana, Shalom – the first high steps set off an electric current running up those long fine legs, swinging the chassis, nipping the waist, pushing out the breasts and illuminating the gaze, beneath toques and bonnets by Prudence, of women who felt themselves adored.

Next year ('Vive la Bagatelle') we'd got the message – now our eyes were prepared – we saw an hourglass silhouette but somehow Vivienne had removed the false bum and bust.

this woman understands form. And she understands woman. She sees woman through a woman's eyes: she seems to see her through men's eyes, too. Her women are audacious, flirty, sexy and feminine – and never commonplace. What I find so marvellous about Westwood's clothes is that they always lend themselves to the woman to express her mood, her caprice, and the choice gives beauty to her intelligence. They are about potential. Vivienne Westwood's women are truly chic.

Concerning my friend Vivienne, I have never met anyone more giving and generous. She has given fashion a new language and vocabulary. She has given us a rare look into the artistic process and into the vision of one of its giants. She has taken us on a marvellous voyage and if she ever felt she'd had enough I would ask them to dim the lights on the Eiffel Tower and play 'God save the Queen'.

TATLER

April fool

£

his woman was
once a punk

SEE PAGE 104

0263 716000

Handsome John Rotten L.T.D.

A
TRUE
STAR
OF OUR
TIMES
MAAAN!

A SeX PiSTOLs HERO

worlds end

WESTWOOD

VIVIENNE

ORN IN ENGLAND

enne Westwood
alcolm McLaren
te

CE CODDINGTON

he
ds End Collection
mn - Winter 81 Show
e Pillar Hall Olympia
0 for 1.00pm
day 31st March

"WITCHES"
VIVIENNE WESTWOOD et MALCOLM McLAREN'S
WORLD'S END COLLECTION L'HIVER '83
R.S.V.P. SYLVIE GRUMBACH, 17 RUE DE VERNEUIL, PARIS 75007
TEL: 296 34 81 + 246 10 87
COUR CARRÉE DU LOUVRE SALLE LESCOT
21 MARS 1983 à 18H
SHOWROOM
à L'HOTEL EDOUARD VII, LES 22 ET 23 MARS 1983

Chronology

1941   8 April, Vivienne Westwood is born Vivienne Isabel Swire in Glossop, Derbyshire. She moves with her family to London at the age of 17.

1970   Vivienne Westwood and her partner, Malcolm McLaren, open their shop Let It Rock at 430, King's Road, Chelsea. They sell Fifties records and memorabilia and design teddy-boy and Fifties-inspired clothes.

1972   Too Fast To Live, Too Young To Die. McLaren and Westwood change the name and shop decor each time they present a new collection. They now design rocker-style clothes and zoot suits.

1973   Designs the costumes for Ringo Starr in the film *That'll Be the Day*.

1974   Fashion designs feature S&M clothing and T-shirts with pornographic texts and images. McLaren and Westwood are prosecuted under the obscenity laws. The shop's name and decor change again, this time to Sex. Vivienne Westwood designs clothes for the New York Dolls.

1976   Seditionaries. McLaren and Westwood launch punk fashion. McLaren launches the group the Sex Pistols.

1981   World's End. The shop at 430 keeps the name and decor to this day. First catwalk show, the 'Pirate' collection, London. McLaren launches Bow Wow Wow, the controversial pop group fronted by 15-year-old Annabella.

1982   'Nostalgia of Mud' collection. McLaren and Westwood show in Paris, the first English designers to do so since Mary Quant. Open first central London location shop, Nostalgia of Mud, looking like an excavation site, selling 'Buffalo Girls' collection. McLaren works in conjunction with the Webo Girls on his 'scratch', New York influenced dance music.

1983   The collaboration between McLaren and Westwood ends. Their work had been gradually polarizing since the 'Pirate' collection; hers has concentrated on fashion, his on music. 'Witches' collection – hugely influential giant nylon macs, training shoes on the catwalk. Working with Keith Haring's graffiti art.

1984   'Best of Five'. Vivienne Westwood is invited to show in Tokyo with Hanae Mori, Calvin Klein, Claude Montana and Gianfranco Ferre.

1985   'Crini' collection: short crinoline; platform shoes.

1987   Vivienne Westwood returns to London after an absence of 5 years to show her 'Harris Tweed' collection. Introduction of 18th-century corset reworked for ready-to-wear.

1988   Davies Street shop opening.

1989   John Fairchild of *W.W.D.*, in his book *Chic Savages*, rates Vivienne Westwood one of the six best designers in the world. She is the only woman included.

1989–91   Guest professor of fashion at the Vienna Academy of Applied Art, where she meets Andreas Kronthaler whom she later marries and who now designs with her.

Vivienne Westwood, wearing a dress from the 'Five Centuries Ago' collection, Autumn/Winter 1997. Hair by Aldo Coppola. Photo Gian Paolo Barbieri.

1990 Vivienne Westwood has always designed menswear which had been sold with her women's collections. She now shows her first menswear collection, 'Cut and Slash', in conjunction with Pitti Uomo in Florence. *The South Bank Show*, ITV, one-hour profile; she is the only fashion designer to be featured on this programme.

1990 & 1991 Awarded British Designer of the Year Award two years running.

1991 Vivienne Westwood is chosen to show in Tokyo with Christian Lacroix, Isaac Mizrahi and Franco Moschino at The Fashion Summit. Returns to Paris to show her 'Dressing Up' collection on the invitation of Azzedine Alaïa. Designs costumes for the Royal Ballet Gala entitled 'Carnival of the Birds', performed at the Royal Opera House.

1992 Is made Honorary Senior Fellow of the Royal College of Art. First influence of 20th-century couture, especially Dior, appears in her work. CAPC (Centre d'Art Plastique et Contemporain), Bordeaux, France: A retrospective défilé, 20 November. In December, presented with the OBE by HM The Queen. Introduction of wedding gowns.

1993 The first fashion designer for Swatch, Vivienne Westwood creates two watches, 'Putti' and 'Orb'. 'Anglomania' collection; vast press coverage as Naomi Campbell takes a fall in 'super-elevated' shoes. These shoes become the most popular exhibit in the Victoria and Albert Museum. Creates her own tartan, Mac Andreas, which is recognized by the official museum of Lochcarron.

1994 New silhouette, extreme feminine shape with 'faux cul' foundation: the new power dressing.

1995 Designs costumes for the film *Leaving Las Vegas*.

1996 Designs all the costumes for the production of *The Threepenny Opera*, by Bertolt Brecht and Kurt Weill, performed at the Burgtheater, Vienna. Designs costumes for the opera *Hamlet*, with music by Ambroise Thomas, performed for the first time in London after 100 years. Launch of Men's collection entitled 'Man', shown in Milan. Japanese flagship shop opening.

1997 London, Conduit Street flagship shop opening. Launch of 'Red Label' collection shown in London on girls as young as thirteen. Launch of 'Anglomania' street style collection.

1998 September: Perfume launch.

'Les Femmes ne connaissent pas toute leur coquetterie' collection, Spring/Summer 1996. Gemmilliana exits in a gown with 'Watteau' back while Kate Moss takes to the catwalk. © Jean Larivière.

Vivienne Westwood

Vivienne Westwood was the first punk. Photographed in 1976 against the interior walls of the shop Seditionaries, she wears a muslin top with the slogan 'Destroy'. Photo Norma Morrisseau.
Vivienne Westwood impersonates Margaret Thatcher for the cover of *Tatler,* April, 1989. © Michael Roberts. The Condé Nast Publications, Inc./ *Tatler.*

'Les Femmes ne connaissent pas toute leur coquetterie' (Women do not realize quite what flirts they are). La Rochefoucauld's maxim was the title of a Spring/Summer 1996 collection inspired by the frivolity and flirtation of the 18th century. Linda Evangelista wears a green taffeta asymmetrical 'Watteau' gown. © Guy Marineau. Vivienne Westwood wears her plastic bag as a rain hat, 1994. © Inez Van Lamsweerde/ Vinoodh Matadin/ A+C Anthology.

Vivienne Westwood photographed in 1971 in the interior of the shop Let It Rock at 430, King's Road, wearing a yellow mohair sweater, black tights and winklepicker boots. Photo David Parkinson. Courtesy Vivienne Westwood.
Johnny Rotten wearing black cotton sateen bondage outfit. The photograph was taken in the Sex Pistols office in 1975. In an idle moment Rotten added the graffiti. Photo Ray Stevenson. Courtesy Vivienne Westwood.

Vivienne Westwood and friends photographed outside the shop Let It Rock in 1970. Courtesy Vivienne Westwood. Too Fast To Live, Too Young To Die. Malcolm McLaren and friend Gerry Goldstein in 1972 outside the new shop front. McLaren and Westwood changed the name and shop decor each time they presented a new collection; they were now more heavily into rocker-style clothes and zoot suits. Courtesy Vivienne Westwood.

Jordan and Paul Getty, shop assistants, outside 430, King's Road, now called Sex, 1974. The shop, with its pink plastic padded shop sign and sponge covered interior walls sprayed with graffiti, sold S&M clothing and T-shirts with pornographic images. Courtesy Vivienne Westwood. 1976: McLaren and Westwood launched punk fashion and changed the name of the shop to Seditionaries. It became a target for attack by skinheads. Courtesy Vivienne Westwood.

The shop 'World's End' is suggestive of a ship, with its small windows, low ceiling and sloping floor. It dates from the 'Pirate' collection of 1981; the clock with 13 hours which goes backwards belongs to Vivienne Westwood. Courtesy Vivienne Westwood. Invitation to McLaren and Westwood's first fashion show, the 'Pirate' collection, 1981. Photo Andy Earl. Courtesy Vivienne Westwood.

The 'Pirate' collection of 1981 marked a turning point in the work of Vivienne Westwood. She began to explore the cut of historical garments, as can be seen in the full-sleeved shirts; the jacket, trousers and waistcoats are developed from 17th-century tailoring. There was also a strong influence of ethnic cuts and themes in this collection. The squiggle print is taken from an African woodblock. Photos Robyn Beech.

'Nostalgia of Mud' collection, March 1982: ethnic Peruvian inspiration, muddy colours, twisted and asymmetrical cuts, bra's as outerwear, oversize hats with dents. Catwalk shows were presented in London's Olympia and in Paris at Angelina's Tea Room. © François Lamy.

Invitation to the 'Witches' fashion show, 1983. Courtesy Vivienne Westwood.
The 'Witches' collection of Autumn/Winter 1983 concentrated on ethnic cuts. Vivienne Westwood wearing grey melange knitwear from the collection.
© Courtesy Vivienne Westwood.

'Harris Tweed' collection, Autumn/Winter 1987. Inspired by the fashion from the period when the Queen was a teenager. Sara Stockbridge wears red velvet 'Stature of Liberty' corset and mini crini (the mini crini was designed in 1984) and 'Rocking Horse' platform shoes; hairstyle created by Vivienne Westwood. Photo Kim Knott. **Sara in Harris tweed crown.** © Nick Knight.

'Voyage to Cythera' collection, Autumn/Winter 1989. Inspired by Watteau's paintings, in particular those of the Commedia del Arte, Harlequin and Colombine. Photo Robyn Beech.
Harlequin tights combined with Savile Row look: velvet jacket, shirt worn half undone, tie loose. This look was sometimes presented with nude tights.
© Sacha/*Marie Claire* UK September 1989/*European Magazines.*

Nude tights with green mirror fig leaf from the 'Voyage to Cythera' collection, Autumn/Winter 1989. Photo Steven Klein. © The Condé Nast Publications, Inc./ British *Vogue.*
'Pagan I' collection, Spring/Summer 1988. Christy Turlington wearing cream silk jersey draped 'Stature of Liberty' corset. Photo Peter Lindbergh. © The Condé Nast Publications, Inc./ British *Vogue.*

'Portrait' collection, Autumn/Winter 1990. Corset with photographic print of Boucher's *Shepherd Watching a Sleeping Shepherdess* from the Wallace Collection. © Karl Lagerfeld.

'Dressing Up' collection, Autumn/Winter 1991. Corset with photographic print of baby's face (portrait by Frans Hals) worn on the catwalk by Suzie Bick. © Roxanne Lowit.

Detail of inlay design on the back of a mirror by the furniture craftsman André-Charles Boulle. © The Wallace Collection.

'Portrait' collection, Autumn/Winter 1990. Vivienne Westwood wearing a black stretch velvet sheath with placed design in gold foil reworked from a design by Boulle; stole with photographic print from a Boucher painting; court shoes with concealed platform. © Anthony Crickway.

'Harris Tweed' collection, Autumn/Winter 1987. Red barathea suit with black-buttoning jacket and black velvet collar. Photo Snowdon. © The Condé Nast Publications, Inc./ British *Vogue*.

'Voyage to Cythera' collection, Autumn/Winter 1989. Tatiana Patitz in Bruce of Kinnaird tartan suit. *Vogue* cover: Photo Peter Lindbergh. © The Condé Nast Publications, Inc./ British *Vogue*.

'Anglomania' collection, Autumn/Winter 1993. Christy Turlington wearing ensemble of mixed tartans. Tam-o'-shanter by Prudence. © Mario Testino/The Condé Nast Publications, Inc./ British *Vogue*.

'Anglomania' collection, Autumn/Winter 1993. Famous photo of Naomi Campbell falling down. Royal blue velvet jacket and tartan kilt, cream rubber stockings, blue snakeskin super-elevated courts (now in the Victoria and Albert Museum). © Sipa Press. 'Anglomania' collection, Autumn/Winter 1993. Linda Evangelista in mixed tartan Highlander ensemble. Tam-o'-shanter by Prudence. © Courtesy Vivienne Westwood.

Luccio Lucciano in burgundy wool and dark green satin stripe double-breasted suit, Man Collection Autumn/Winter 1996. Photo Inez Van Lamsweerde. © Courtesy Vivienne Westwood. **'Storm in a Teacup' collection,** Autumn/Winter 1996. Sybil Buck in brown chalkstripe single-breasted jacket and trousers in taupe pinstripe; brocade waistcoat and shirt and tie in same striped poplin. Bowler by Prudence. © Terence Donovan with kind permission of Mrs Diana Donovan.

Pourpoint coat. This padded garment entered fashion worn with a low jeweled belt and long hose. Musée des Soieries de Lyon. © Courtesy Vivienne Westwood. **Camelhair coat** from the Man Autumn/Winter 1996 collection. This demonstrates how close to an original historical garment Vivienne Westwood is prepared to go and how ready she is to reveal her sources – otherwise the coat would seem entirely modern. © Assouline.

'Erotic Zones' collection, Spring/Summer 1994. False bottom comprising wire cage attached to pull-on elastic foundation. Frame made by the father of Andreas Franz Kronthaler, who has a forge in the Tyrol. © Michael Thompson.
'Vive la Cocotte' collection, Autumn/Winter 1995. Nadja Auermann wearing a red cashmere suit over a foundation with padded breasts and false-bottom cage. Hat by Prudence. © Niall McInerney.

Selection of dresses from 'Erotic Zones' collection, Spring/Summer 1995. Extremely feminine silhouettes created by false-bottom cage. Hats by Prudence. Photo Steven Meisel for American *Vogue*. © Steven Meisel/A + C Anthology.

'Vive la Cocotte' collection, Autumn/Winter 1995. Demi Moore wears 'Queen of Sheba' dress inspired by pagan themes in Tiepolo's paintings. Dress embroidered in beads and ostrich feathers by Pearl. © Outline Demi Moore.

Greg Hanson wears a beaded jacket entitled 'Martyr to Love', from the Man Autumn/Winter 1996 collection. Jacket constructed over a corset and embroidered in beads by Pearl. © Ugo Camera Press.
Luccio Lucciano wears a host's gown cut on pourpoint lines in black crepe marocain, Man Autumn/Winter 1996 collection. © Inez Van Lamsweerde/ Vinoodh Matadin/A + C Anthology.

'Vive la Bagatelle' collection, Spring/Summer 1997. Naomi Campbell in draped column of violet marocain. © Niall McInerney.
Katja Simon wearing a dress in gold shot cream duchess satin. From the 'Vive la Bagatelle' collection, Spring/Summer 1997. Headdress by Prudence. © Niall McInerney.

'Cafe Society' collection, Spring/Summer 1994. Vivienne Westwood and Andreas Kronthaler photographed in the Wallace Collection. Grand rustic dress in orange and yellow shot taffeta with tulle gypsy blouse and raffia straw petticoat. © *Elle*/Jean-Marie Périer.

Andreas Kronthaler wears a black cashmere and sheepskin coat inspired by a painting by Holbein, Man Spring/Summer 1997 collection. Hat by Prudence. Photo Gian Paolo Barbieri. 'Five Centuries Ago' collection: 'The Queen and her Punk'. Jerry Hall wears a cream duchess satin dress with a design of exotic animals copied by Fabric Frontline from a dress belonging to Elizabeth I. Autumn/Winter 1997. © Gian Paolo Barbieri.

The publishers would like to thank the house of Vivienne Westwood and most particularly Vivienne Westwood, Sarah Matthew, Asiya Durrani and Murray Blewett.

Gratitude is also due to Demi Moore, Jerry Hall, Lord Snowdon, Karl Lagerfeld, Eric Pfrunder, Steven Meisel, Mario Testino, Inez Van Lamsweerde & Vinoodh Matadin, Michael Thompson, Roxanne Lowit, Jean Larivière, Niall McInerney, Guy Marineau, Robyn Beech, Ugo Camera, François Lamy, Kim Knott, Anthony Crickmay, Linda Evangelista, Naomi Campbell, Karen Mulder, Christy Turlington, Nadja Auermann, Shalom Harlow, Tatjana Patitz, and to Sybil Buck.

Our thanks in particular to Maud Molyneux, Mrs Diana Donovan, Nathalie Dewulf (*Marie Claire* – France) and Rosanna Sguera (Art + Commerce).

Finally, this book would not have been possible without the invaluable assistance of Ruth Eagleton (The Condé Nast Publications Ltd), Catherine Joint-Dieterle and Philippe Fort (Musée de la Mode et du Costume – Palais Galliera), Catherine Legros (*Elle*/Scoop), Joanna Charlton (The Wallace Collection), Jamie Cabreza (Roxanne Lowit Photographs Inc.), Martine (Sipa Press), Emma Wheeler (Nick Knight), Shirani (Art Partner), Arno Adida (Outline), Laurent Rojot, Sabine Killinger (Elite), and Turly Productions Inc.

Our thanks to them all.

Catch a Falling Tortoise

PAUL McDONALD

Cinnamon Press
Independent Innovative International

Published by Cinnamon Press
Meirion House, Glan yr afon, Tanygrisiau,
Blaenau Ffestiniog, Gwynedd LL41 3SU
www.cinnamonpress.com

The right of Paul McDonald to be identified as author of this work has
been asserted by him in accordance with the Copyright, Designs and
Patent Act, 1988.
© 2007 Paul McDonald
ISBN 978-1-905614-22-6
British Library Cataloguing in Publication Data. A CIP record for this
book can be obtained from the British Library.

Designed and typeset in Palatino by Cinnamon Press
Cover design by Mike Fortune-Wood from original art-work 'Catch' by
Sasha Radosavljevic, agency: dreamstime.com
Printed in Great Britain by Biddles Ltd, King's Lynn, Norfolk